SILVER SERIES OF GROWN-UP WISDOM

Bertha Baggage

Janet Snyder and Kathleen Canova

Published by
Hasmark Publishing International
www.hasmarkpublishing.com

Copyright © 2024 Janet Snyder & Kathleen Canova

First Edition

No part of this book may be reproduced or transmitted in any form or by any means, electronic or mechanical, including photocopying, recording or by any information storage and retrieval system, without written permission from the author, except for the inclusion of brief quotations in a review.

Disclaimer:
This book is designed to provide information and motivation to our readers. It is sold with the understanding that the publisher is not engaged to render any type of psychological, legal, or any other kind of professional advice. The content of each article is the sole expression and opinion of its author, and not necessarily that of the publisher. No warranties or guarantees are expressed or implied by the publisher's choice to include any of the content in this volume. Neither the publisher nor the individual author(s) shall be liable for any physical, psychological, emotional, financial, or commercial damages, including, but not limited to, special, incidental, consequential or other damages. Our views and rights are the same: You are responsible for your own choices, actions, and results.

Permission should be addressed in writing to Janet & Kathy at janet@storybookpath.com

Cover Design: Anne Karklins [anne@hasmarkpublishing.com]
Interior Layout: Amit Dey [amit@hasmarkpublishing.com]
Illustrations: Tim O'Connell

ISBN 13: 978-1-77482-292-0
ISBN 10: 1-77482-292-X

Dedication

I dedicate this book to my young adult self because at the time I carried ALL of Bertha's emotional baggage. The neighborhood is an interpretation of my childhood community and I love it still. Therefore, I equally dedicate this book to the Germantown/Schnitzelburg Neighborhood in Louisville, KY USA

Additionally, I dedicate this book to my illustrator and grade school classmate/friend, Tim O'Connell, even though he initially said, "This story is kinda' dark." Thank you for bringing Bertha to life with your pencil, interpretations and creative talent.

Drum roll please for my last dedication, Kathy Canova; a visionary who happens to be one of my dearest friends, high school classmate, and now business partner. Kathy envisioned something bigger than Bertha and together we created the Silver Series of Grown-up Wisdom, illustrated storybooks for 'Big Kids.'

Acknowledgements

In gratitude for the unconditional love, encouragement, and support we've received from our **families** ~ those we were born into as well as those we helped create.

In gratitude for our dear **friends** who've been on this writing journey with us, especially those who have continued to coax and cheer us onward for years.

In gratitude for our brilliant **behind-the-scene creative duo**, Kimberly Lauersdorf and Kristan Clark, with candid critiques, enthusiastic readings, and challenging prep-talks.

In gratitude for the **crowd-funding** opportunity through BackerKit, and especially Lafia Morrow's leadership, laughter and navigation of this innovative financial pathway.

In gratitude for the **co-publishing** partnership with Hasmark Publishing International, especially its Founder, Judy O'Beirn's personal buy-in of this project and Jenn Gibson's capable leadership and coordination of their talented team.

In gratitude for the **lived experiences** we write about, because life is definitely not a spectator's sport; and we're proudly battle-tested warriors, now stronger, wiser and more compassionate having traveled these roads.

In gratitude for the **faith and freedom** to be true to ourselves, willing to tell bold stories, the good, the bad and the ugly; truly a legacy project for our culturally-relevant times.

In gratitude to **The Maker of Heaven and Earth, The Divine One** who introduced us to each other as teenagers, so that we could ultimately fulfill our life's purpose these many decades later, creating works of art and entertainment that will inspire humans forever.

In gratitude of our banner, **Silver Series of Grown-Up Wisdom**, a divine gift that we hold sacred, as we commit to creating and nurturing a genre of those "becoming" and "being" grown-up. It has been said, "it takes a village" to raise a child; and we believe that holds true when raising up "big kids" too. May our thought-provoking, illustrated short stories for grown-ups warm the hearts and minds of our beloved readers, and flourish for many generations.

Bertha was in familiar company as she sat with the other regulars in her favorite neighborhood pub.

Some came to socialize. Everybody knew everybody here.

Some came to drown their problems; enough liquor helped them forget.

Bertha came to let her opinions be known. Bertha brought her baggage.

She blamed the government for her feelings of scarcity. It was so much easier to cast blame than to deal with the underlying emotions of unworthiness.

Bertha laughed, joked, and made fun of the others who *"talked about their feelings."*

She didn't want that *"feeling vomit"* coming up around her.

Bertha was not at all comfortable having a vulnerable conversation.

Alcohol works wonders to hush our emotions and keep them hidden deep down inside.

Bertha lived in the center of a German Catholic community.

Her modest home was small but efficient and easy to maintain. The house had tiny yards which she manicured, front and back.

In her neighborhood, most of the backyards featured a painted statue of The Blessed Mother Mary wearing a blue and white robe. She stood surrounded by marigolds, varieties of bright yellow and orange colors. And Bertha's backyard was no different. Bertha's German heritage was embedded deep into her veins.

Bertha loved living in this little house because she grew up in this neighborhood and knew almost all her neighbors.

Bertha attended and graduated from the Catholic school, St. Heineken, which was just around the corner. But at this stage in her life, she especially loved the little pubs in the neighborhood.

It was so convenient to walk and grab a nice cocktail or cold beer! Don't all Germans love their cold beer?!

Bertha was attractive and charismatic. Her nose was always lightly powdered, and she wore red lipstick. Bertha's clothes usually looked pleasant on her sturdy, strong-framed body.

Her hair was brown with lots of curly rings surrounding her face.

But boy! That Bertha, she carried around a lot of baggage.

Bertha spent her days downtown in a large business office with lots of other women. Her department handled most of the typing and filing and she was their supervisor. This position afforded her enough money for her mortgage and the essentials for living.

However, Bertha didn't enjoy her job, nor did she get a sense of accomplishment performing it.

"That's why they call it work," she would exclaim. "It's not supposed to be FUN. Life's a Bitch and then you die!"

Although Bertha was cordial to her co-workers, she stirred up a lot of drama inside her department. Bertha was highly amused when some of the women had petty little disagreements and she loved stirring that pot. And then this toxic little game always gave Bertha something to talk about with her friends at the bar.

What Bertha didn't fully understand was that her own unresolved issues with her emotionally and mentally abusive mother was actually the culprit of all her baggage. For unknown reasons, Bertha had been the "chosen child" for her mother's rage, frustration, and wrath during her childhood.

So, Bertha was quite comfortable circulating drama throughout her work environment because it was familiar. She stayed in the familiar where she felt most comfortable.

This was the fuel that helped her carry out her mission for her daily office amusement.

There was one young woman in Bertha's office that didn't feed into all the drama and gossip that Bertha circulated. This young woman got under Bertha's thin skin.

Sometimes when Bertha walked through the front door of a pub, the bartender could tell by the look on her face that she was bringing baggage into his bar. Those nights, he would prepare lots of Bertha's favorite cocktails!

She would start spewing, "Well, I'm just sorry if I'm not as thin and trim as the gal at work. She gets on my nerves acting all happy and shit. I can't stand a bubbly morning person! There's definitely something wrong with her!"

That night, Bertha had lots of cocktails.

Whatever triggered her reaction to her co-worker would not be allowed to come up as she poured alcohol down her throat.

Others would talk about their crappy, happy, morning co-workers and all agreed they were a bunch of idiots.

They chuckled with each story that was told.

As a young girl, Bertha was an athlete and she loved the sport of slow-pitch softball. She played third base for the community team sponsored by her favorite neighborhood pub and bar, Checkers Pub.

Bertha could hit the crap out of a softball and directly into an open space, easily getting base hit after base hit.

She was always at the top of the batting order, and boy, could she ever snag a hard ground ball and fire it over to first base to get an OUT!

It was here, on the playing field, where Bertha most enjoyed her time and where she made lifelong friends.

She carried very few bags with her at game time, but nowadays, Bertha heads directly to her favorite pub for a cold brew, and she seems to be pulling quite a load.

On this night she was triggered by running into an old team player who brought her mother and best friend to the local pub.

Their close mother/daughter relationship seemed more like a sisterhood, and they genuinely enjoyed one another's company. Bertha resented their friendship, and even though she'd never admit it, she was jealous!

The alcohol flowed with ease as she avoided dealing with these disturbing, painful feelings and emotions.

It was getting late when Bertha met Dan's eye on the other side of the room. He was another regular at the bar and a regular with Bertha too.

She was usually disappointed in herself the day after they had a rendezvous, yet Dan always seemed to show up when Bertha was in a state of drunkenness.

Dan eagerly came over and started flirting with Bertha, and she melted into his words, staring into his attractive blue eyes.

Sizing up the situation, Dan seized an opportunity to have a sex partner that night, and he took Bertha home.

Dan always let Bertha know just how smokin' hot they were together. But Bertha was deeply frustrated after each episode because Dan didn't call, and not once had he taken her out on a date—not even to dinner or lunch, for that matter.

Bertha had been married once. She complained that he was a low-life with a drinking problem and he carried around a lot of rage. The last time he came home drunk and mistreated her, she lugged his baggage on the porch and sent him away! Before that, Bertha had endured 20+ years with this man.

She claimed every problem in their marriage was **his** fault and told anyone who would listen to prove her point.

"I was good to him. But do you think he appreciated me?!? Oh, hell to the NO! That scum left his dirty clothes all over our cute little house. And, I could barely get the meal on the table before he gulped it up, sometimes slurping like a wild animal!"

There must have been a shitload of baggage piled up in that little house when Bertha's husband lived there. His baggage, her baggage. Everywhere you look, baggage, baggage, baggage!!

If those bags had labels, they would read: *Unworthiness, Scarcity, Low Self-Esteem, Anger, Resentment, and Jealousy.*

Yet, Bertha continued to frequent all the local pubs.

It was fine because she knew almost everyone and was welcomed by all the regulars at the local pubs.

When it was Bertha's time to talk, she talked and talked. "I am through with men! They are scum and every one of them is an ASS! I can't think of one thing I need from a man!! I'm certainly not going to take care of some nasty old fart that doesn't give two shits about me!!"

I betcha, deep down, Bertha wanted the love of a man in her life, but she wasn't even capable of self-love. One of the big bags she carried around was packed with unworthiness. Alcohol, it seemed, filled that void, and her bar friends rallied around her.

Bertha could count on her bar buddies to meet up at the local watering hole any night of the week. And, they sometimes organized group outings to their favorite local college ball games.

Football season was their favorite and the most fun because they spent hours in the lot outside the stadium, drinking their adult beverages, sharing food and conversation, all the while complaining about their crappy jobs and strange family members.

Yep, Bertha's baggage always came along for the day, even on those fun football outings.

The office wasn't the only place Bertha stirred up drama and circulated gossip. Remember, it was very familiar territory.

Every Tuesday evening, St. Heineken Church sponsored a Bingo night in their large basement complete with cold beer and popcorn.

Bertha and some bar regulars were also regular weekly Bingo players.

Since they were all superstitious, they obtained the same table and sat in the same chairs, week after week.

In between Bingo games, their favorite conversations were about other acquaintances—out of ear shot, of course.

From time to time over the years, Bertha would mourn the passing of one of her regular bar friends.

The story always seemed to be the same. They would reminisce, "Remember that nice man that sat at the end of the bar every night? He got a grave illness and died just a few short months later. May he rest in peace."

When their friend was laid out at the community funeral parlor, they all celebrated his passing with a cooler full of cold beer right out there in the parking lot. It was a Catholic ritual and tradition they always honored.

They stayed for hours and drowned their sorrows and staggered around the baggage they brought along for the wake.

Alcohol seemed to work wonders in every emotional situation, and Bertha was comfortable and familiar with this solution.

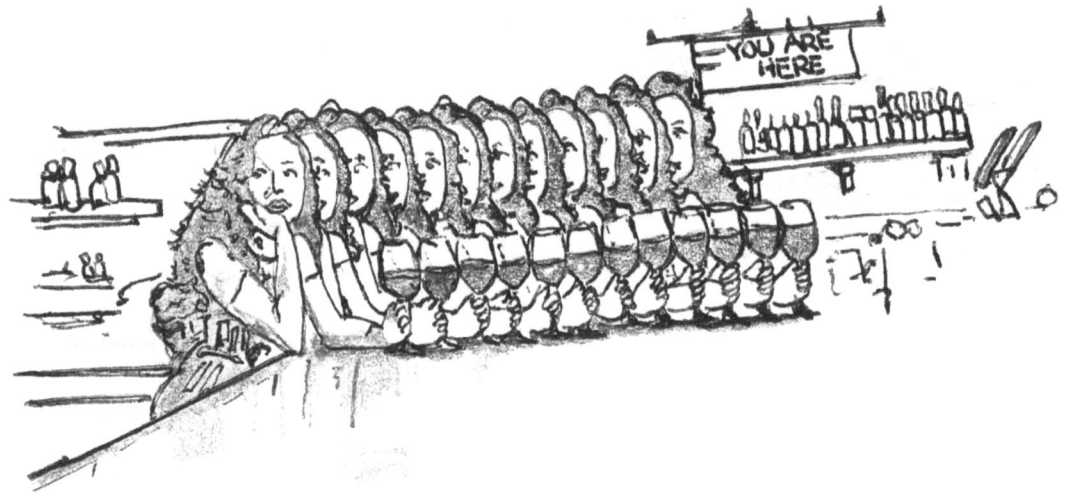

Bertha would go about her usual routine day after day, month after month, and year after year. She worked, took care of her home, and continued to frequent the local bars.

One evening at Bertha's favorite beer joint, she agreed wholeheartedly with someone's comment.

"LIFE is FLYING BY, way too FAST! How long have we been coming here, y'all?!"

"Thirty years!?!? No shit! Boy, life really is flying by, my friends!"

I'm sure you could sit with someone like Bertha today, have a drink or two, and hash over excuses for being stuck in a stagnant routine.

You could listen to the denial and witness the practice of conformity.

Bertha didn't seem to believe in herself and couldn't see herself prosperous and flourishing.

As Bertha visited her usual thought patterns, she also stayed stuck in her familiar, comfortable, and negative state of being. Yet, she sometimes wondered if and when things would change. Perhaps, then, she could find some happiness.

Life just wasn't fair to Bertha!

WE BECOME WHAT WE THINK ABOUT, and in Bertha's situation, she couldn't get away from her own baggage. That's a DAMN SHAME.

When excessive drinking is used as a coping mechanism, like in Bertha's case, it can cause many emotional and physical health problems. You CAN find building blocks to a life of hope and a better future. By making the most of yourself, you make the world a better place to live.

Give yourself permission to take a new path. All you need is the plan, the road map, and the courage to move forward.

Join the 30-Day,
Entry Level program for Personal Development.

We provide heartfelt, entertaining, real-life stories of adversity about the challenges of overcoming the after-effects endured from psychological and emotional childhood/young adult trauma.

Free Introductory Guidebook, *'OOOH Crap!*
WE BECOME WHAT WE THINK ABOUT'
when you sign up at
WWW.STORYBOOKPATH.COM.

Meet the Authors

Janet Snyder, is the creator of *StoryBookPath.com a 30-day personal development program* and eBook designed to help you discover and live the life you love and desire. After finding her enthusiastic, authentic voice and true strength from her own personal struggle with the negative aftereffects endured from mental and emotional childhood/young adult trauma, Janet's fulfilling her life purpose of helping others.

Also, Founder of *StoryBook Cottages*, she uses her well-earned degree for interior design and her vivacious love of the earth designing playhouses constructed from recycled materials and sustainable living green rooftops. Janet is the mother of three and a "Nan" to her grandchildren who also live in her hometown of Louisville, Kentucky.

Kathleen Canova, successful entrepreneur and founder of the Canova Group, LLC, has facilitated and educated many regarding domestic crisis intervention, including deep emotional and spiritual healing practices. Rooted from her own lived experiences, and after extensive training and certifications, she shares her heartfelt hope, passion and inspiration with humankind.

Living in Westminster, Colorado near her adult children and grandchildren, who affectionately call her "Yaya," she enjoys spending quality time with family and friends when she's not reading, writing and traveling.

Sales Page

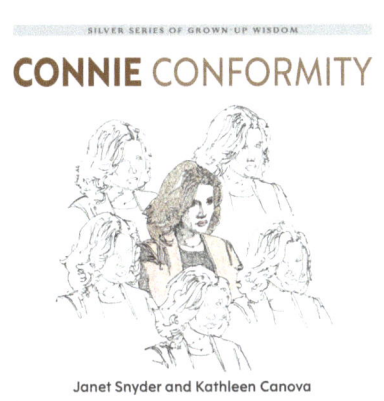

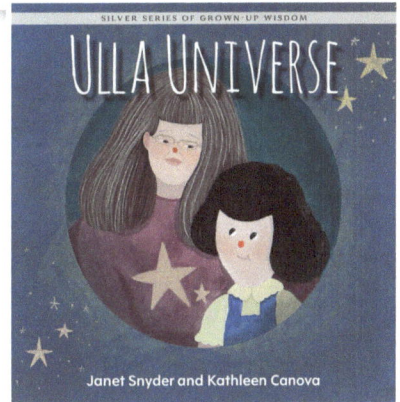

First-Time Co-Authors:

Janet Snyder and Kathleen Canova

Available on Amazon and Ingram-Spark now

www.storybookpath.com

On FACEBOOK: STORYBOOKPATH & SILVER SISTERS WISDOM

janet@storybookpath.com & kathleenkarrercanova@gmail.com

www.ingramcontent.com/pod-product-compliance
Lightning Source LLC
LaVergne TN
LVHW071031070426
835507LV00002B/117